Flame Dancer

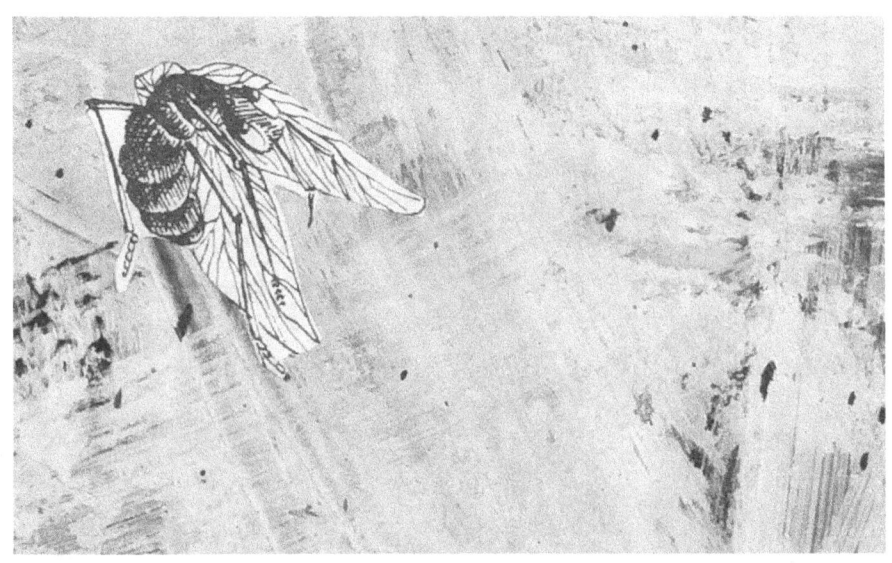

poems by

Nancy M. Fisher

Plain View Press
P.O. 42255
Austin, TX 78704

plainviewpress.net
pk@plainviewpress.net
512-441-2452

Copyright © 2011 Nancy M. Fisher. All rights reserved under International and Pan-American Copyright Conventions. No part of this book may be reproduced or distributed in any form or by any means, or stored in a data base or retrieval system, without written permission from the author. All rights, including electronic, are reserved by the author and publisher.

ISBN: 978-1-935514-02-2
Library of Congress Control Number: 2011925849

Cover art: *Fly Abstract* by Julie K. Jack, MFA
Cover design by Pam Knight

Acknowledgements

Poems in this collection have appeared in the following publications: "Cadmus" in *TETYC*, 1980; "Maintenance Man" in *TETYC*, 1978; "Malthus' Gun" in *TETYC*, 1976; "Myrtle Beach" in *TETYC*, 1977; "Stratford" in *TETYC*, 1994; "Coleridge's Aeolian Harp" in *NeoVictorian/Cochlea*, 1996; "Kafka's Castle" in *The Sow's Ear*, 1991; "Lighting the Fire" in *Wind*, 1980; "John Milton Visits Galileo" in *Broken Streets*, 1983; "Pageant" in *Advent Thoughts*, 2002; "Sabbath Elevator" in *Deronda Review*, 2009; "Spider at the Station" in *Sunday Suitor*, 1998; "Flying Blind" in *Chattanooga Writers' Project of the Arts and Education Council*, 1985 and "Trash" in *Troubadour*, 1999.

"Only Connect. . . ."
E. M. Forster

Contents

Family   9

The Maintenance Man	11
Father	12
Father's Day	13
Dandelions	14
Treasure Trove	15
T-Ball	16
Little League	17
Arsenic and Old Lace	18
Springtime	19
Abelard	20
Machines	21
Unclean	22
Drown Proofing	23
Cleaning the Gutters	24
Landscaping	25
Myopic of Ear as Eye	26
The Organ	27
Sherry	28
Wedding at Shakertown	29

Community   31

Cadmus	33
Nurse June	34
Faculty Dream Club	35
The Cancer People	36
The Yellow Bus	37
The Gym at Jellico	38
Malthus' Gun	39
Wadlow Gap	40
Eastman Corporation	41
Local Muse	42

Myrtle Beach	43
Oshkosh	44
Trash	48
Seasons	49
Neighbors	50
Spider at the Station	51
Tulip	52
Pilings	53
Double Pane	55
Trapping Squirrels	56
Early Frost	57
To Mourn the Fallen	58

World   59

Over the Alps	61
John Milton Visits Galileo	62
Dracula's Castle	64
Kafka's Castle	66
Pilgrimage	68
Stratford 1993	70
We Murder To Dissect	71
Coleridge's Lime Tree Bower	72
Sulis Minerva	73
Dachau	74
The Sabbath Elevator	75
The Empty Pyramid	76
Flame Dancer	79

God   81

Pageant	83
Lighting the Fire	84
Ghosts	85
Gethsemane	86

Holy Island	87
Cuthbert	88
Festival of the Venerable Bede	89
The Vatican	90
Michaelangelo's Moses	91
Michaelangelo's Pietas	92
The Bread of Life	93
The Prodigal	94
Flying Blind	96
The Gulls	97
Ash Wednesday	98
About the Author	99
About the Cover Artist	99

Family

The Maintenance Man

He shares in my dilemma and my passion.
We both must value polished sinks and floors.
The very walls would suffocate without him
as skin would stifle but for sustaining pores.
He always calls to me from down the hall
and shows his grandson's picture for his part.
Somehow my husband always keeps me waiting
while he lets Susie push his cleaning cart.
His eyes smile past us to his occupation;
he cleans each cranny, checks on each machine.
No better does a forest strew pine needles.
No scavenger picks carcasses as clean.
Physicians keep the body in good order,
and priests use prayers to grease our gritty souls.
Hard wear makes calluses on hands, or blisters;
with these psychiatrists mend fractioned wholes.
Has any good come, but it asks for better,
and asking, runs the circle where it can?
The only interest great as preservation
of self, is species. God too is a maintenance man.

Nancy M. Fisher

Father

> *for Malcolm McWhorter*

Before he died, my dad got into rocks,
bringing us samples he had gleaned from dirt,
his whole collection cradled in one box.
When he was only two, so small and pert,
his mother found him playing with a snake,
just out of sight, digging in the sand.
She beat the creature off with a garden rake,
I'm told.   I saw a bird eat from his hand
when he held out a crumb. The creature came
up to our picnic table, my children, slight
and rapt and still, watching his spirit tame
timidity, even as St. Francis might.
In death, I feared to look upon his face,
so calm it was, so full of human grace.

Father's Day

Albuquerque, New Mexico 1988

On Father's Day they were admitted free:
Father—grandfather now—son and his papoose
at the Indian Cultural Center in Albuquerque.
We lunched on beans and squash, sipping our juice,
then watched, in the blistering sun, the ceremony—
the buffalo and soaring eagle dance,
spectacular as any performed by Cherokee.
Besmeared with paint, bedecked with feathers, prance
the warriors in their male initiation.
Scouts' honor—all our sons seek manhood here,
forest or desert, city or reservation.
It is a ritual no female may come near.
What has a mother to do with sons? Squaw
like Mother Earth with her own daughter-in-law.

Nancy M. Fisher
Dandelions

I wandered lonely as a cloud …
      Actually, we were driving down the turnpike.
When all at once I saw a crowd …
      and I did not even see them …
          "Look, Mom!"
          "Where? What?"
A host of golden …
      Dandelions—the whole field, yellow!
         and I didn't even see them …
"Oh, Mom! Did you ever see anything so beautiful?"
      And I hadn't even seen them …
For oft, when on my couch I lie …
Couches are made for potatoes, these days,
      eyes processing nostalgia movies …
In vacant or in pensive mood …
      What happens when the gold is gone,
when cotton puffs fly in the wind, reseeding?
      Will my grandson see the dandelions?
I do not find solitude bliss.

Treasure Trove

"A treasure trove," he called the jewel box,
thinking of pirates and Wendy and the lost boys;
thinking of him is one of my last joys
even as I sort his grandfather's socks.
A treasure trove? What's really there? Some rocks
sequestered in silver, earrings of olive wood
from Bethlehem—no—one was lost. A rood
from Cuthbert's cathedral. I lost the broach from Scot-
land too. I have the turquoise ones his dad
brought me from Venezuela, but I wear
the diamond that filled the box that Christmas day.
Why keep a single earring, half a pair?
I do not need it to remember the lad.
The more love grows, the more's to give away.

Nancy M. Fisher
T-Ball

We came at six to watch our grandson play
T-ball, the game for kindergarten kids
where no one pitches, no one slides the way
the big boys do. Here girls play too; their bids
as equals yield adjustments—sugar and spice.
The biggest problem's their attention span.
The man on first has missed his catch now, twice,
for playing in the dirt; one cherub ran
but stopped to adjust her wayward helmet; next batter
slings down his bat, despite the warning calls.
Ambling toward first base as if it did not matter
this runner's safe because her pursuer falls.
Oh let us love these children, let them know
the world is waiting to welcome their next throw.

Flame Dancer

Little League

They're swaggering now, all twelve, some small, some tall,
but chewing and spitting, even if it is still gum.
They've come a long way from that first T-ball,
climbing the ladder to manhood, rung by rung.
We've watched him warm the bench, year after year,
but not this season: he's found a catcher's fit.
He hit a double, caught a foul ball! Let's cheer
the lad, all padded, catcher's mask and mitt.
There's one thing missing: his beloved Papaw.
More faithful than we ever were, he came.
But when they tried to mend his heart, we saw
how stamina plays out—the final game.
It's not this inning we root for, precious grandson:
the game of life is waiting to be won.

Nancy M. Fisher
Arsenic and Old Lace

The body in the window seat's our grandson;
his mother worries at the need for air.
We scan for air holes, see that there are none,
and settle in our seats. A trumpet's blare
and "Charge!" return us to the plot we saw
some forty years ago, before our son
was even born. You've seen it? Here's the law
having tea with two sweet ladies; no one
suspects they've buried a dozen gents
down in the cellar.   What have we buried since
we saw this play, what memories, what woe?
The jokes, the comedy, they're still the same.
We play our parts, some lively, mostly tame,
and come full circle. Of course! On with the show.

Springtime

The daffodils are sprouting green,
      the winter's growing old;
forever springtime's born anew,
      the single crocus gold.

How many winters have we left,
      my own true love and I?
Enough, this spring has come again,
      so let the winter die.

Tomorrow may not come again,
      but while this day shall last,
I'll whisper to tomorrow's child:
      Seek the future in the past.

Nancy M. Fisher
Abelard

Why do you think of Abelard? Why now?
The fact that they were buried, flesh and pale
bone, is it? I have said I want to blow
in the wind, cremated; buried, if at all
in a small box—-ashes to ashes. But you?
Our almost fifty years would seem too few?
There's space among the pine trees if you wish,
tryst for eternity, shadow and mist.
But every morning, waking, breathing—truth
be told—I am content, my heart's desire.
I'll take a box beside you, but I'm loathe
to search for souls in that slow smoldering fire.
Oh let our children do with us as they will;
let it not fester, lest the thinking kill.

Machines

I run machines—for dishes, words, and clothes.
One washer shakes, the other gapes and croons
of gleaming glasses, china and silver spoons.
My favorite was a combo, heaven knows …
My wee one watched her blankie tumble dry,
its porthole rolling suds, and finally fluff.
Thus she learned patience; I, never enough …
I program images extracted from the sky
and order games for him—*her* little son,
tough little guy, who needs his blankie still …
And what machine is out there that will fill
his images, his future? What will run
his private passions? What machine can bind
the images that feed, that fill a mind?

Nancy M. Fisher
Unclean

"Zach, have you washed your hands? " He shook his head.
"You need to, honey, every time you go."
"My daddy doesn't, Nannie," the child said.
I couldn't help but frown. "You should, you know."
What do you say to a child who answers thus?
Did you know that in *Matthew, Mark,* and *Luke*
the Pharisees complain they never wash
their hands before a meal? All three agree!
If they lived now, I guess they wouldn't flush,
either. Ritual for the Pharisee
told Jew from Gentile, gentleman from jerk.
I understand "unclean" meant something more,
two thousand years ago than it does to us,
but I have trouble seeing past Pasteur.

Drown Proofing

They had their lessons in a private pool,
heated, expensive, but better than the Y.
Drown proofed, she promised; they would learn how cool
it was to swim, how easy not to die.
Ironic, you start with a dead man's float,
come up for air, gasp once, and go back down.
You can go on like this for hours; a boat
can do no better—the life you save, your own.
Is it like that at Easter? *Mark*'s scriptures say
the women found the tomb stone rolled away.
"Go now, I'll join you later in Galilee."
The women left, told no one, left in fear.
Just down from Jerusalem is the Dead Sea;
the Jordan deposits all its savor there.

Nancy M. Fisher

Cleaning the Gutters

a love poem

It's not just the gutters, it's wet packed leaves on the roof.
We should have done them in the fall, but you
were having surgery; your shoulder knew
its limits, now your body reckons proof.
I climb the ladder as I've seen you do
with rake and extended broom; I fear I'm through
before I start. And yet, the leaves come down
turning to mulch already, and there are limbs
aching to topple, tumbling to the ground.
The winter's mild, the noonday sun just skims
the towering treetops, arching toward evening. Past
dying, the daffodils are making haste.

Landscaping

We've lived in woods so long, we find it hard
to do the things that must be done for yard
and shrubs. I mean, how can we cut the grass
when that means killing clover, Queen Anne's lace
and those blue flowers whose name I never knew?
Just yesterday we weeded the flower plot,
intending to spread the cover, but they grew
by morning, shoots and sprigs of God knows what.
The stuff we're putting down should stifle weeds,
allowing light and water to penetrate,
but nothing else; we cover that with mulch.
I don't mind watering the plants so much.
We've planted lilac and heather and other such.
Even the lawn could use some extra seeds.
Wild we prefer, but here we cultivate.

Nancy M. Fisher

Myopic of Ear as Eye

Before penicillin, I remember pain—
hot brick for heating pad, clutching my ear.
Infection runs its course, and my ears drain,
spilling hot fluid, thickening the healing fear.
Bereft of hearing, would memory suffice
to conjure up Segovia's guitar?
Pity the oyster, muscled and blind as ice,
mere mollusk secreting his rare, nebulous scar.
An insect maiden seeks her mate by pitch,
dolphins by sonar, bees by patterns of light.
Myopic of ear as eye, our senses itch
to weld a world past pleasing, past delight.
Would this explain Beethoven's last complaint,
his human voices melting past restraint?

The Organ

With other junk, we took it to the dump;
end over end it fell into the muck.
White sea gulls circled skyward or lined the hump,
and a lone dog dodged the 'dozer's slimy suck.
It was my mother's—soft sounds she played by ear—
but stored first in a barn, then in a shed.
I brought it home, hoping to save the gear
from past to future, living from the dead.
A craftsman, my lover promised that its wood
would make fine furniture, its golden sound
become electric, fine speakers and keyboard
renewed, its varnish stripped, its finish found.
Memory will not outlast its final key.
Buried, its music is forever free.

Nancy M. Fisher
Sherry

for Karen

How little I have shared with you, my daughter,
how little I have known of you and yours.
I'd like to know you've found the living water
and felt the presence—spirit, bird that soars
beyond us. Now you come to say goodbye
to one whose friendship you have shared for years.
A stroke—an aneurysm—what? To die
and leave you nothing but your pool of tears
to drown in. She had a daughter and a son—
now grown—to mourn her, and a sister. You
are friend—only—and yet you are the one
she tried to reach at the last. "Strew
On her roses, roses and not a spray
Of yew"—a poet said that—and I pray …

Wedding at Shakertown

Pleasant Hill, Kentucky

It was our nephew's wedding in Shakertown;
the groom wore a kilt, the bride a Tartan plaid,
splashed sash, over her flowing gown.
The father of the bride—colonel, retired.
I've never seen bridesmaids dressed in black,
but so they were, their flowers purple and white.
Such pleasure it is to witness this holy rite,
the preacher's voice assuring this holy pact.
This morning we listened to a Shaker choir,
a lecture explaining the ways of Shaker folk;
no trinity, they honored a different yoke:
Equal the sexes, in the coming of the hour,
when God the father and mother are as one.
Oh, bless this marriage till their time is done.

Community

Cadmus

For Greg Cowan

"According to tradition, Cadmus brought the alphabet to Greece, and the Greek alphabet is in fact derived from a Phoenician script."
—Encyclopedia Britannica

Warring like dragon's teeth
professors clashed;
        so Cadmus came

between an oral and a literate world,
        slaying dragons in ghettos,
        dispelling myths,
        dispensing sanity.

Ah, literacy never comes with ease,
but takes its toll in sanctimonious
snobbery and smug self-righteousness.

Jogging a country road,
he was slain by an unnamed dragon.

How shall we sow the dragon's teeth without him?

Nancy M. Fisher

Nurse June

Her world was white as winter, warm as wind,
painless as aspirin, softer than a bandage.
Bringing bruised fingers or hearts for her to mend,
students would seek the clinic as a refuge.

For hearts and minds and bodies, young and old,
she was always there, dispensing humor and pills
or movies on VD or the common cold.
The spirit giveth life, the letter kills.

Faculty Dream Club

At lunch we share a dream club,
though we seldom appear in one another's dreams.

Tennis on roller skates,
dragging at beards, the net between them—
colleague and dancer/daughter;

or mine with fingers sprouting in the palm,
or climbing out of windows onto ledges,
or houseboats sinking,
or files ejecting folders like slot machines.

Between our personal and professional lives,
dreams sift out sanity like sand.

My worst by far was a bodiless head,
indulging in intellectual orgies.

Nancy M. Fisher

The Cancer People

The Cancer people sponsored the talent show;
we've wiped out smallpox, and God knows we've tried
as hard with cancer as with polio.
Ours was a tribute to the Beatles' pride,
John Lennon's dirge—songs like "Strawberry Fields,"
as lively as "Sergeant Pepper" and as lean
as Eleanor Rigby's intrusive world. What shields
sanity better than a "Yellow Submarine"?
A world gone wild, in cells and on the street—
cancer and bullets both explode inside
where diamonds and countless stars succor the sweet
songs of our loneliness in hearts that hide.
How long can fame withstand the pious gun?
How long this cancer plague our naked run?

The Yellow Bus

The yellow bus winds down the country road,
blinking first yellow, then scarlet signal lights.
Despairing, I watch the line of children load.
They climb toward knowledge dreamt by Faust, such heights
as even Mephistopheles never sold.
I rode just such a bus once, shivering and pale,
reading romantic tales of love and gold,
of Coleridge's albatross, Keats' nightingale.
The house the children come from is no less
than mine was then, but now with a satellite dish.
The hill behind the house grows kudzu flesh.
The child wears jeans, not my starch stiffened dress.
The bus will take them far from home, it may
yet take them to the stars, oh blessed day.

Nancy M. Fisher

The Gym at Jellico

Jellico, Tennessee

I stepped into the gym at Jellico
and found myself transported back in time,
the scene from nearly forty years ago,
when I, a girl, cheered basketball; now I'm
teaching their mothers, a little early for class.
What can I see in this, a high school game,
so far removed from intellectual tasks?
I watch in wonder, wondering how I came
so far—professor, scholar; once I was
like them—screaming, cheering, bouncing for joy!
Their mothers—taking college courses—pause
amid their household chores to (just think) toy
with skills and knowledge Plato would admire,
except, of course, they're women who aspire.

Malthus' Gun

"How do weeds get so tough?" my son asked me.
His hoe came slacker as the sun came hot.
"It's the only way to survive in the world they've got.
Nobody loves them: tough they have to be."
That goes for people too, the really tough
grow up in slums and learn to steal from us,
the pampered ones who fight square and don't cuss.
Weeds, 'possums, crows, rats, floods, droughts—all fight rough.
We've got to make our population shrink
or God will strike down with Malthus' gun.
"I can't tell weeds from flowers," says my son,
"Tobacco, onions, even tomatoes stink."
God doesn't weed his garden, oh my child.
Our only hope is the flowers that grow wild.

Nancy M. Fisher
Wadlow Gap

They're moving mountains, without an ounce of faith.
The great machines push, plow great rocks and trap
truckloads of dirt for ransom. Wadlow Gap
bridges Virginia and Tennessee; a map
shows one thin wiggly blue line across its face.
We watch them, wait our turn to pass; the pace
is monstrous slow, houses have fallen, bathed
in dust, cavernous boulders tumble past.
The hillside's sprinkled with abandoned cars.
The houses that hang on, hang on to hills,
their driveways spiraling, plumbing a depth that kills
the spirit, that blackens any hint of stars.
And yet last evening I saw the moon come out,
our headlights testing the curves of this new route.

Flame Dancer

Eastman Corporation

Kingsport, Tennessee

We came to learn the process and the drill
by which our earth and air are rendered pure.
Once Kodak, now amorphous, plastics still,
they offer this their environmental tour.
Four fathoms deep and bubbling froth and air,
the process works with gravity and lime,
bugs chewing chemicals in their own lair—
purging—and yet it looks no more than slime.
Last stop—the incendiary—"We burn trash."
Another lecture, OSHA standards. I doze.
The company's concern must be with cash,
but hazards are consumed with fire. Now goes
the hell itself, of liquid, solid waste.
We part with bottled spring water, Heaven's own sweet taste.

Nancy M. Fisher
Local Muse

Weber City, Virginia

I go out walking, looking for a poem,
like Frost or Wordsworth, seeking for a prize,
and so I find it, what's before my eyes:
A man, felling a tree; a woman come
to pick up trash; trees lifting limbs to heaven,
awaiting spring in naked beauty pressed.
The road climbs upward, smooth, tarred and kissed
with sunshine, blue on blue, like silk sheets woven.
At the crest the vista widens, into view
come churches, shops, the highway heading north.
Now winding down, I find no fork to choose,
no choice but face the traffic: trucks overdue
and speeding, past the funeral home and forth
to finish the circle, pay homage to the muse.

Myrtle Beach

1962

The season of green peppers fills the markets
and boardwalks crawl like stubble showing face.
They shuffle past dreamlike, beach-burned, unkempt:
Strangers, yet welded to one time and space.

Where sweet potatoes and curved palmettos ripen
from Hattaras to Myrtle lie the wrecks.
Drunk with popcorn and apples the crowd converge like cards
while strides the blind man through their tumbled decks.

His eyes were streaked with blankness like lined paper;
his wife, though blond, no deformed virtue showed;
the cup on his guitar shivered as he strummed,
and their small child hopped between them like a toad.

The shops stay open; converse on corners, twist
girls in skin white shorts, black shirts, and bubbled locks
(a world where only art and time bear order,
where moved the soul to seeking); where tick the clocks

to regulate the rides: glee stricken faces
inhabit ostrich wings and flesh filled baskets
turn wheels to tumble; stars shatter into prisms
lined bright as jeweled darkness inside caskets.

A 1910 mechanical band organ
like Proust's smooth sculptured past, playing box nine,
insists its presence—ballerinas twirling
on blue-gold carvings which naked cherubs line.

Molecular movements *en masse* bear some prediction;
a smaller number lessens certainty;
(only art makes sense) life's loose ends dangle;
we saunter down the boardwalk blind as he.

Nancy M. Fisher
Oshkosh

August 1991

1

We huddled in our tent
counting the seconds
from flash to thunder.
One . . . two . . . .
six is a mile away.
The tent was lit like daylight.

2

The T-Shirt read: "Bladder problems?"
"You can have it if you'll wear it!"
And I did, a walking billboard.
They were selling hard plastic liners
for the Cessna bladder tank,
the one that failed us
with its wrinkled water pockets.
Anyway, we lived to tell the tale.

3

Curtis Pitts
"I thought he was god,
but if he was,
he'd do something about the weather."
So toasted the singular pilot of the Little Stinker.

"He was a pilot, not an engineer."
Like the hummingbird,
they said it wouldn't fly—
silly looking contraption, double winged.
What Leonardo only dreamed of, he flew.

4

Jim Bede
Until now, we'd only seen the pictures—
    fat, squat, ungainly, the Bede 5.
Its flesh is no more handsome,
    but its sibling—
this bearded man *is* an engineer.
The kit he's building now is supersonic—
from your basement to the heavens—
the Bede 10.

5

Stealth Fighter
The fighter was roped off appropriately,
    stealth cardboard,
        black and boxy textured surface.
Sleek silver aluminum
    invited deadly rockets,
        but this our champion ...
We never lost a one!
The pilot accepted the roses
    for the triple crown.

6

Wandering the aisles
    admiring the engines
we fell into conversation with a German salesman.
His was a turbo diesel
    astounding among conventional
        Lycomings and Continentals.
Meanwhile, the air show had begun,
    with simulated bombings
        on the flightline.
"The noise is far too great," he told us.
"The pilots should be detained in labor camps."

7

Flying Tigers
Where is Homer when we need him?
    As many as thirteen gathered,
        including a widowed nurse
            who'd flown the Burma Road
with the flying tigers.
I knew them only from film,
    John Wayne assaulting the skies.
"They went out as boys," she said,
    "but they returned as men."
Oh, but the tales they might have told.

8

USO Dance
"Wear your uniform and your dancing shoes."
After the accolades for Desert Storm
the Air Force Band struck up Glen Miller tunes.
We danced, but in the space of a narrow aisle.
The heroism had not been our war.
For ours, there was no cause to celebrate.

9

On the flightline,
the warbirds were everywhere.
I'd never seen a ball turret before,
nor the Flying Fortress
sporting its women and trophy flags.
I understand the Enola Gay
—its space reserved in the Smithsonian—
has been rejected.
I haven't seen the wall in Washington either,
nor the Arizona.

10

The Cessna Party
The Cessna Party was at Motel Six:
"We reserved the room
when it was only a sign on an empty lot."
Beer and bratwurst,
sauerkraut and corn—
ears sizzling in their husks.
Even the coming of rain dared not dampen us.

Nancy M. Fisher
Trash

Is it because we're near a tavern, or
our road's a shortcut to nowhere we get
so much? Beer cans and colas I forget
but tonight's collection I cannot endure:
A bag from Wal-Mart, an empty box, Fact Plus,
a pregnancy test, no less; last week,
a condom, spent and discarded. Such things reek.
A country road's become a toilet's flush?
I hadn't thought of it before, but here
last summer, starving, covered with ticks, she strayed
onto our doorstep—too old now to be spayed.
Her hair is matted still, but the ticks are gone.
"God don't make no trash." Lewis's *Mere*
Christianity sustains as life goes on.

Seasons

The road we walk each day forbids no trespass.
Last fall, just as the crisp cold air set in,
we saw a dog, its carcass in the grass,
and left it undisturbed. And so its twin
came out to greet us each and every day—
live, barking, raucous—brown lumbering thing,
not threatening, really; it was only its play,
to frolic with humans intent on staving
off ravages of time. We walked that way
all winter. Frost, then snow, and there it lay.
Spring came, the thaw, then maggots had their run.
By summer, only the bones remained; the sun
bleached what was left, and when the mowing machine
swept through the right-of-way, they scattered clean.

Nancy M. Fisher
Neighbors

Digging through the garbage, we find their name
on an envelope among the plastic jars;
milk cartons, styrofoam containers frame
the space they dumped their refuse from their cars.
Our squirrels do not complain about the trash,
neighborly even with our construction debris.
"And will you prosecute?" the officer asks.
Indeed we shall. Above the site, a tree
has fallen, rotten, under its own weight.
We spent last weekend digging out the roots
of healthy trees, lest they too share its fate.
We set out onions and tomato shoots,
and from another tree, we cut barbed wire.
Across the creek, at dusk, the sun's on fire.

Spider at the Station

I saw the web as I was pumping gas,
its spider patient in its intricate space;
I've seen them in the forest, in the grass,
but never in so greasy a public place.
Remembering Robert Bruce from a childhood book,
I will not violate its precious trap
and set the nozzle gently on its hook.
Pursued, he crept into a cave, a gap,
so careful to avoid the spider's sieve.
His kindness saved him! Seeing it undisturbed,
they passed his presence by, letting him live.
The spider awaits the quiver of its prey.
Headlights pierce the darkness. Will we be spared?

Nancy M. Fisher
Tulip

As I nestled the garbage
cans against the trees,
I marveled at the
solitary tulip sprouting in harm's way.
Tonight, as I collected the empty cans
it blossomed, untrampled,
magnificent
yellow streaked with red like an unborn chick.

Pilings

> *Knoxville, Tennessee 1988*

Arriving mid-afternoon,
        we open the strip tease curtains
                to unveil
a mosaic of motion—
        the soundless music
                of a construction site.
Staring,
        you can begin to see
                the musical score:
bright orange propane tanks; a welder's arc;
        red hard hats, black,
                like checkers across a board.
And at the center is the moving crane,
maestro whirling its circular baton,
its arm eight stories high.
Intricate as the Rosetta Stone,
alive as Bosch's Temptation of St. Anthony,
the scene is vibrant as the mind itself.
The earth is diked with wooden walls
and beside the revolving crane,
a little man is shoveling spoonfuls of dirt.
We identify a lesser machine, a drill,
vomiting its ruptured anthill,
searching not water nor oil but rock and air.
Oh, the crane is pounding a piling now,
its concrete cylinder dropped, lifted, pounded.
The very earth shakes at each letting go.
You have to stare to make out anything.
        Ah yes, there is a completed section
squared, graveled, girded with plastic and wire.
It is ready for concrete mud.
            The pilings there are finished, their metal rods
                    sprouting like flowerless stems.
Suddenly—"What in the world?"—the crane
        plants truck tires over an empty pile.

Nancy M. Fisher

Soundless it shudders—quivers—dynamite!
From the street you can see nothing:
      fenced toilet maybe, trucks, wheelbarrows,
certainly not the little man's spoonfuls of dirt.
By evening, our rented curtains closed against the night,
      I wonder how deep our pilings go to bedrock
before the morning steels the structures of our souls.

Double Pane

Like Dostoevsky's double, the bird attacks
our window, challenging the cardinal who slides
into the duel joust. What coward hides
therein? Again, it flutters, shudders, cracks.
When the bird perches, it can see within,
but when it backs away, the mirrored bird
usurps its territory yet again.
We watch its antics bemused—deceived, absurd.
Last spring a squirrel nested in our attic,
gnawed her way in, chewed the louver clean through.
Repaired, it was attacked again. Frantic,
we shot the creature with our twenty-two.
Through a glass darkly, we stare, yearning to know
where mirrors lead, where myriad spirits go.

Nancy M. Fisher
Trapping Squirrels

There in the ceiling, the two holes remain
where insulation fell like cotton, like snow.
Rejecting violence, we did not go
the murderous route to rid us of this bane.
The man who sold the traps warned us of this:
A squirrel left untended would die of fright.
And so we loaded sunflower seed at night
and freed the frantic creatures to alien bliss.
Displaced, the refugees would dash away
and scurry up a tree. I've counted six,
or is it seven now? We'll miss their tricks
straddling the feeder, monitoring its sway.
We saved them. All but one. That morning when
I simply forgot. Omission too is sin.

Early Frost

The early frost has ravished our neighbor's wood;
our woods fared better, cautious to the last.
The leaves are shriveled, brown, misunderstood.

It's hardly fair, as if their fate were cast,
malignant forces bypassing the rite of spring.
I'd rather wait till fall to see the past

come forward, watching walnut and maple fling
scarlet and gold across the meadow's span.
We've not put out sunflower yet, nor seedling.

Our hawks have perched as high as any can,
screeching their war cry, even as they feed their young.
On our porch, a sparrow's nesting above the fan.

So many voices, such courage in their song,
against this war, how can I hold my tongue?

Nancy M. Fisher
To Mourn the Fallen

VFW Athens, Tennessee, May 2001

There were no jets this morning in the sky
to mourn the fallen, only clouds and rain.
Inside, we heard their names read, the refrain
rounded with rhetoric, Wilfred Owen's old lie—
Virgil's before him—*It is sweet and fitting to die
for one's country.* So many names—the chain
lengthening in peace time, echoing the pain,
from Flanders Field to Desert Storm they cry.
And yet, the living, here and now are fed
sweet ham and cheese, salad, German bread.
Ingrid, our German bride, as a young child saw
Hitler himself; a citizen now, her awe
humbles us. Our anthem sung now, taps said,
the bugle sounds—we mourn the living dead.

World

Over the Alps

On the plane from Athens to London
we gaped at the Alps and talked:
"And you were born in Delphi?"
where yesterday I had walked.

The hills are ragged at Delphi
like the hills of Tennessee.
"I've always dreamed of England
where everyone is free."

On the plane from Athens to London
our conversation was brief,
but stealing home from Delphi
I hoard her home like a thief.

Nancy M. Fisher

John Milton Visits Galileo

Florence, Italy 1638

When Milton spoke to Galileo in Florence
already he imagined Samson pulling down the temple.
He was a young man then, only thirty.
It was before the revolution, the beheading, the restoration.
He was not yet blinded with celestial light
nor envious of Adam nor bewitched by Eve.
He would not go to Sicily or Greece,
only to Florence with ghosts of Michelangelo and Dante.

They spoke in Latin, sharing the music
of the spheres they inherited from their fathers.
Proud of his Protestant heritage,
Milton pledged to smuggle manuscripts to Holland.
He would remember this before the House of Commons, urging
free speech, the power of truth to win through free inquiry.

"Would you not like to pull down columns of this church that
holds you in contempt—that stifles freedom,
that enslaves its subjects?"

But Galileo shook his massive head.
"The church moves slowly.
We do not need the violence of revolution."
John Milton was to remember these words, years hence.

"But the corruption! Even in England
we have moral decadence—but here—
the idolatry, the opulence of Rome."

"I never objected to opulence."

"The more's the pity, sir."

Youth sees with different eyes.
Moses' eyes are never David's, even in stone.

"Ponder the heavens.
They dwarf our petty vanities."

"And so I shall. And so I shall."

Nancy M. Fisher

Dracula's Castle

Romania 1987

Imagine a country bounded with barbed wire,
with manned guard towers and mines in no-man's land.
Crossing the border requires some little patience,
and petty bribes, two cans of Michelob.

In Transylvania, the tourist bureau has designated
Bran Castle as Dracula's—a tenuous connection—
Vlad the Impaler was once imprisoned there.

The castle itself is spectacular enough—up, up, you climb.
There's a passageway up a secret flight of stairs;
there are ramparts, crevices, a well.
There are no bats in daylight,
only the musty odor we encounter in unsealed basements.

We came by way of Cluj, through countryside
where peasants harvest wheat with sickles
and barefoot children welcome gum from tourists.
A speeding ticket, a stop to look at embroideries
held high by peasant women under the bus windows.
They handed our driver fistfuls of local currency,
and he brought out his grab bag full of coffee.
The local guide sold belts and vests of velvet.

In Brazov stores display print dresses draped on hangers
aligned with chalk faces and legs on the window panes.
On every corner were lottery sales and ice cream.
A friend's suitcase was stolen that very evening,
lifted right off the sidewalk by a passerby.

Flame Dancer

At dinner we shared a table with three locals;
the girl, a housewife, spoke impeccable English:
"There is nothing to buy, nothing.
So we come and drink.
Cigarettes are simply not to be had."
She took a last drag on hers, snubbing the half inch butt.
"I hope to visit my sister in Canada," she paused, "forever."

"It's not as bad as all that," a pale one interjected.
The husband, a furrier, nodded resolutely.
"I have no relatives in Canada."

Count Dracula does not need to sleep in daylight;
the streetlights come on only after curfew.

We slept badly that night; the air was suffocating.
Though my flesh crawled, I only saw one flea.
Even now, my throat is still constricted.
Leaving, they mirror each passport against our paling faces.

Nancy M. Fisher

Kafka's Castle

Prague, Czechoslovakia, 1987

Unlike the "Metamorphosis," he never finished it.
Less sinister than *The Trial*, K had connections
by telephone, by word of mouth;
an architect, he had been promised work.

Guidebook in hand, we set out to explore his city.
In Prague it rained all morning
and we took shelter first in the subway,
then the museum—rocks and stones and diamonds,
butterflies and skeletons of elephants.

By noon the rain let up and we found a beer garden
serving pork and sauerkraut so sweet it fairly melted.
Why is food never pleasant in his stories?

Right after lunch we found the Jewish ghetto,
twelve-layered cemetery, stones sprouting like lilies in mud,
stone buildings blazing with the star of David.

Entering the synagogue is time past—
high gothic windows, scrolls, embroideries;
an upper room has drawings from death camps.
Not till mid-afternoon did we set out for the castle in earnest.
You could see the spires in the distance above the city.
"Take Streetcar 12," the hotel clerk had said.
Before we knew it, it went right past our plaza.

When we got off, the spires were no longer in view.
We began to climb in that direction,
past open basement windows with cabbage cooking,
past children playing in sandboxes and mothers reading.

Flame Dancer

The path continued higher, promising, promising,
up a flight of stairs overhung with branches,
smelling of flowers new washed with morning rain.

As we climbed, steeper and steeper,
the city expanded behind us, barges and bridges,
docks and clear-flowing water.
Suddenly we saw it, flag fluttering:
An unexpected embassy, our own.

Then there was a wall, a fence with tangled barbed wire.
Now even Kafka found such barricades.
There is no entrance at all, not even guards.

At the plaza we met another couple
who had indeed climbed all the way to the castle.
"There's nothing there," they said. "A church."

Back down the mountain we followed the trolley lines.
Down cobble stones we found a store with plum brandy
and across Charles Bridge, artists selling sketches
beneath the magnificent dark statues of Catholic saints.

Nancy M. Fisher

Pilgrimage

Canterbury, England

I.

The week was one for rain, and there for us
outside the hotel, the red Frames Richards' bus.
Like Chaucer's pilgrims we were on our way
to Canterbury for a touring day.
"You goin' to Leeds Castle?" came a voice.
"To Canterbury."
          "Yes, the same tour choice."

          So we met Ollie, visitor from Down Under,
and we three planned a splendid day of wonder.
How's that? No stories? Do not be absurd.
We didn't have to make up what we heard.
Her daughter was a banker from Singapore
in London for six weeks to learn the score.
She'll only stay two weeks, but in that time
she'll get to Wales and Newcastle on the Tyne.

          But now the bus sets out in earnest from
the central office where we've had to come.
A tour of London? Brief: The Tower, Thames.
We walked this way just yesterday it seems.
And now the bus heads south, or is it east?
Three days it took the pilgrims, three at least.
Our first stop was Leeds Castle, just a filler,
remodeled unauthentic, turret to cellar.
They're big on Henry here, and Henry's wives,
divorced, beheaded, only one survives.
How beautiful the portrait of the daughters;
how elegant the black swans on the waters.
Why, here first Begin and Sadat did try
before Camp David where they the knot did tie.
Why could not Hank and Tom reach an accord
before the king was careless with his word.
"And who shall rid me of this meddling priest?"

Flame Dancer

Four lusty knights—so we are told—at least.
      But now we make our way to Canterbury.
Why must the driver persist in such a hurry?
We didn't even get a pot of tea
or to the museum where dog collars be.
      And so to Canterbury—now we disembark.
"Pay strict attention: return to Longport Park
by three o'clock, and we'll be on our way
to get you back to London by end of day."
      We padded through the streets and came in sight
of the towering spires of the cathedral's height …

      II.

We came to the cathedral half in awe
of history, but visions Chaucer saw
bred frivolity. We left it at the gate.
Inside, it was all stone, all somber, fate
that Henry Tutor sought to overthrow;
he took the bones of Thomas, and with one blow
banished all martyrs, too, the church's lands
and filled the palace coffers, his own hands.
Where once the coffin stood, a candle's flame
like Christ's own tomb, empty but for a name.
Roped off are areas where tourists file;
construction moves apace, they lay new tile.
The plain glass windows have not been replaced,
yet none compare with what has been defaced.
Following the route of tourists, at last we find
the vestibule to temper our peace of mind:
A corner of modern martyrs, a candle ring.
Thomas was but the first, now Gandhi, King …

From blessed Canterbury we made our way
past Dover's sheer white cliffs at end of day
and back to London, in the pouring rain.
I shall not chance to trace this path again.
Descend we must into the cavernous way,
down, down, to rise again, weary at Chelsea.

Nancy M. Fisher
Stratford 1993

for Lisa

We came that evening in the gentle rain.
Lisa, the lawyer, had never read the play
we saw that evening: Portia, modern, plain.
Fair Lisa, learn of love and law this day.
In modern dress, with steel, computers, and glass,
the Jew—a Babbitt or Willy Loman—fell
for Portia's fancy flattery, beguiling lass.
How can we not admire the bard's hard sell?
Daughter and ducets, he loses all through greed.
Tragic? In mimicry we hear the voice
of a fool. And so to Belmont—silver, lead,
or shimmering gold, consider Portia's choice:
Portia admonishes her lover to think on this.
Fair Lisa, claim your lover with a kiss.

We Murder To Dissect

Walking with Wordsworth, I gathered weeds last night:
A purple thistle, a green blackberry (red),
another purple blossom with drooping head,
two kinds of clover, regal plum and white.
I left untouched the honeysuckle site,
the poison oak, the kudzu and the bed
of cultivated flowers. Home—a dead
handful of flowers wilted, stank. Tonight
I tried the path again, this time withal
remembering. I knelt and fondled Queen Anne's lace—
a cluster—budding green hairy pod for show;
another, opening its blushing, pinkish face;
full open only one—bejeweled snow.
Tonight I left them in their crannied wall.

Nancy M. Fisher

Coleridge's Lime Tree Bower

The group went on to Keswick without me
while I went into Hexham to get x-rayed.
My finger was not broken, they could see
that much; a torn ligament, they said.
Back in the inn, I studied in my room:
"The Lime Tree Bower My Prison," and Coleridge's pain.
His wife had spilled hot milk, and he stayed home
while his friends went walking without him on the plain.
He wasn't whining, sorry to be there;
he catalogued the pleasures they would see.
Their walks would take them to the places where
he knew already—imagination's key!
So shall I rest content, no worse for wear,
rejoicing at the splendid tales we'll share.

Sulis Minerva

Bath, England

Before the Saxons came, the Roman armies
embossed their brand on Britain's furthermost shore—
from Hadrian's wall on the utmost Scottish border,
from the gossamer cliffs of Dover past Salisbury plain.
Of all the sites in England, where to begin?
Here at the waters of Bath, sacred to Druids
from time immemorial. Rome's splendid engineers
harnessed the bubbling swampland and made a shrine
to the goddess—Athena—and called her Sulis Minerva.
How little of her remains—fragments, curses,
a gorgon's head, but more like Sol than woman.
Let us be wary of curses, and witches' wares.
They took us past the steaming sacred spring
and gave us pamphlets explaining the temple precinct—
cold plunges, saunas, tepid swimming pools.
The plumbing was of lead, the ceiling vaulted,
the mosaics under their feet were flaming horses.
One passes through the pump room to the surface,
erupting to the city's cobbled streets.

There street musicians play with open caskets,
their music like perfume from another time.

The Romans had come and gone before the Saxons,
a churlish, slovenly people who neglected the baths,
but Sulis Athena would not rest content
until she had filled the whole land with liberty.

Nancy M. Fisher
Dachau

There are no ghosts among museum pictures.
It is too clean, too antiseptic.
Apparently it was the same in operation.

A checkered bedspread must be arranged just square
or there were penalties.
I saw no trace of heaters in the wooden barracks,
the triple tiered bunks lying side by side.
"Work Makes Free" over the gate; Dante could have used it.

Foundations, numbered are all that line
the rows where barracks stood.
Three memorials and a convent have been added.
The Jewish is black, a pit, with a rising windowed tower;
the Catholic, predictably imposing, cathedral-like.
The Protestant is a complex—chapel, bookstore, reading room.

Behind them are the crematories and the disinfectant showers.
The gas chambers, though never used, still smell of gas.
Victims were hanged on beams before the ovens.

It is all so clean, so sterile.
At least the gravel makes the walking hard.

The Sabbath Elevator

Tel Aviv, Israel

In Tel Aviv the elevator stops
on each floor on the Sabbath. Believers then
can ride and not betray a sudden lapse
of faith, temptation to indulge in sin
to push the buttons.
                From the hall window we
can look out over the Mediterranean Sea.

The elevator stops, and we must fly
to catch it lest we're caught between the floors.
Israelis manage, even as they lie
between Egyptian and Lebanese shores,
to balance faith in God against the odds,
nor Greek, nor Christian, nor Egyptian gods.

Nancy M. Fisher
The Empty Pyramid

    Sadat's Tomb 1985

        I

      Cairo
The tour bus let us out
    where four flat columns are tilted to a point,
      an angled arch—
        the empty pyramid
which rises above the Unknown Soldier's tomb.

Sadat is here.
    There is no grave to rob.
        His presence fills the open space and silence.

Across the avenue
    of taxis, donkey carts, and herds of goats
      is the reviewing stand
where an assassin's bullet cut him down,
    scimitar from the mountains.

His quarters on the Nile stand brown and empty,
    walled from the sounds of Cairo.
The dust from the subway drilling
    settles in flame trees and balconies.

Trucks of raw recruits roll by—mere children.

Off duty, they nap in barracks
    or toss their balls beside the Papyrus Museum
      moored on the river
or keep stiff watch by the Russian Embassy.

The children blossom in the streets,
    in King Tut's chambers:
      "What time is it?"
Saladin raised a splendid Mosque,
    Sadat an empty tomb.

II

Luxor

The train to Luxor traveled by night,
    swaying, moaning down the tracks,
stopping to celebrate the end of Ramadan.
An hour in the station, the chant incessant—
    fasting by day—nor food, nor water,
    nay, nor women nor wine.
Three passages to Karnack—
    asphalt, rail, and that green serpent, the Nile.

The tombs are empty at Luxor,
    carved into mountains like subways
        with brilliant graffiti,
the cartouche of Ramses emblazoned,
    ciphers, rosette-keyed.

There is no one here but tourists and dead kings.
Up river rises Sadat's High Dam at Aswan,
    buttress like Joseph's silos
        against famine and drought.
Desert mountains, caves cracked with secrets,
    there are no pyramids at Karnack,
        only the columns lifting up the sky,
only the sacred lake for purification,
    only the avenue of splendid sphinxes.

III

Jerusalem

Startling the whole world,
    Sadat went to Jerusalem,
        The Knesset, the Dome of the Rock.
Imagine Joseph returned instead of Moses.
    Imagine Saladin and a smiting dove.
        Imagine Christ come to the Golden Gate.

Nancy M. Fisher

The zero in the column is full.
        The streets of the city reject grenades for flowers.
                Israel is making the desert bloom
even as Egypt nurtures the waters of the Nile.

Civilization is green with irrigation.
        The farmers reap their harvest,
                children of Cain.

A bus across the Sinai,
        a ferry across the Suez,
                along the coast to Gaza
where Philistine cities stood
        to Jerusalem.

And did he stand beside the Golden Gate?
        And did he see the sun come up from Jericho?
This time there is no stone to roll away.
        The empty pyramid will erupt
                like a mountain flooded with joy.

Flame Dancer

Jamaica 2008

After the swim, after the rum,
we settled in to while away the morning,
watching the snorkelers,
watching the parasail, the sun worshipers,
dosing, even.

Sand on the beach gleamed golden,
the water crystal cold,
its depth soft peppered with stones.

We had been warned of thieves,
warned to be wary,
but we had been promised
no entertainment at all.

We hardly noticed when he came
strolling up the concrete platform,
positioning his pole waist high,
stripping to the waist himself,
his flesh as tanned as caramel.

We hadn't danced the limbo in thirty years,

but here amidst the palms and sand and sea
he danced, bending back as if
he had no bones at all.

Again and again, he lowered the bar,
his body hinging backwards like a clam.
At its lowest rung he poured the liquid
fluid down the pole and lit it.

There were gasps as he slithered
under the flaming pole,
fluid as the flame himself.

Nancy M. Fisher

Abandoning the pole he lighted flame sticks,
a simple twirling first, then eating fire,
swallowing the stick, spewing streams of flame.

The hot sand should have blistered beneath his feet.

Thieves ourselves, we had no money left to tip him.

Even the camera balked,
its after images as blank as a vampire's mirror.

Flame Dancer

God

Pageant

In seventh grade, I stared into a manger
worshipping no doll, only a stark bulb light,
oblivious to peril, sensing no danger,
our tableau sweetly poised for angels' flight.
Shepherds and wise men, gathering round the mother,
their gifts of gold before the baby's bed.
At the reunion this summer, I discover
that Joseph's no longer with us, his widow's wed.
No one remembered this pageant on that night
and only now it all comes back to me.
They went into the world—a perilous flight,
the route through Jerusalem to Calvary.
So let us live our lives that we may first
give witness to the holiness of Christ.

Nancy M. Fisher

Lighting the Fire

Lighting the fire before the barbecue
we come to that old ritual, the sacrifice:
They did it for their gods, as though they knew

what constituted virtue, and what vice.
The chicken goes on next, the sauce replete
with lemons and catsup and vinegar; the ice

goes in the tub for beer. What piteous feet
once trekked the mountains, as Abraham with his son
to sacrifice upon an altar. Wheat
would do quite well for our gods; Cain's would have done,
what once was unacceptable to the One.

Ghosts

Oak Ridge, Tennessee

Eating my chicken sandwich
    across from the Catholic Church
I watch the ghost cars come out of the trees
    to merge with the real turnpike traffic.
I know it is illusion, windows
    mirroring the rain and treacherous night,
but they flow like a cleansing river
    of light in the ubiquitous dark.

Nancy M. Fisher

Gethsemane

Trappist, Kentucky

What is the proper way to worship God?
In silence, here among the pines.
In Bardstown, in the cathedral, we were told
of the monastery, whose numbers dwindle.
"A monastery, here?" And then it came to me—
"Is this where Thomas Merton … ?" Yes, of course.

Visitors are tolerated, but not encouraged.
The walls are like a fortress, its gates are iron.
Contrary to popular belief,
silence has never been compulsory.
Electrocuted, he was, from a faulty fan,
in the orient, exploring the Zen connection.

Holy Island

Lindisfarne, England

We rode the causeway onto Holy Island
in mist and fog, desolate marsh and mud.
No weapons there, no skillful craft of Wayland,
only the abbey high above the flood.
As pious as St. Francis, stands the statue,
St. Cuthbert humble among the holy stones;
the abbey once was overgrown with virtue,
but now, bereft of even holy bones.
We fed the birds, gulls swooping round the center
where streets run out like spokes upon a ring.
Some caught the crumbs in air, sensing winter;
others alighted, cautious, tasting, testing …
What do they fear? New pirates come to lure
them senseless—wrecked and wretched—on the shore?

Nancy M. Fisher
Cuthbert

Lo, it is written by the Venerable Bede
that Cuthbert took himself to Lindisfarne;
past planting time, but he set out the seed,
past harvest time, and yet he reaped the corn.
We saw him honored in a country church,
a window stained, recording his wondrous feats:
The crows repenting of their curious perch;
his prayers protecting fishermen their fleets.
An angel brought the hermit bishop bread.
The very seas made offering, a beam
to build his church, to weave the slender thread
about his flock—St. Francis he did seem.
The Vicar played us host, a man as calm
as colors feast the eyes, or ears a psalm.

Festival of the Venerable Bede

Durham, England

Fleeing the Vikings, they brought the bones to Durham;
the Normans raised the stones to cathedral height.
Here they might worship, adore the Holy Lamb,
let in his presence, filter his holy light.
We came to Evensong, the Venerable Bede's
festival for singing, voices like angels' breath.
It is his word we take of St. Cuthbert's deeds,
rehearsing the prayer with which he met his death:
I pray you, noble Jesu, that as you
Have granted me to hear your words of light,
To grant the bounty of your wisdom; few
Approach your presence but from dreaded night.
So shall the echo ring at Evensong;
so shall we cherish voices chaste and young.

Nancy M. Fisher
The Vatican

In heaven they'll speak Italian.
I will not care to go.

The rooms are hot and sultry,
the wine cheap, coins rare;
it is hard to render Caesar his in Rome.

The only things worth seeing
were made by a Florentine:
Moses, just down from Il Duce's balcony;
God and Adam, on the quickie tour;
and the reconstructed Pieta, now in glass.

Here Titian, there Raphael,
the Black Pope, the purple throne,
the crucifixes already blessed,

Peter receiving the keys of Rome
or the bust of Caesar smashed,
its pedestal replenished with a cross.

You wander through the corridors,
your belly sweetened with the curds of goats,
past portrait after portrait of the popes.

How can they be so regal, infallible?
Where is the modesty of one like Christ?

But suddenly you come upon a simple stone
as plain as honors any New England grave;
behind it light plays as through a Grecian temple.
Its inscription: In memory of Pope John.

Michaelangelo's Moses

Rome, Italy

Schoolchildren are told nothing if not lies—
had you been here to witness Caesar run
you would not sit so calm as if to rise,
surveyed by giggling youngsters and their nun.
St. Peter's in Chains—this church surrounds the lone
magnificent sculptured marble in your name
four centuries since he found you in stone,
but was your spirit here when Peter came?
Legend of ancient Egypt, Palestine,
striking down Pharaoh's sons, water from rock.
Did you hear lions roar and Christians whine
before he fashioned you from marble block?
Unlock your secret—magic that first blow
when Moses sat for Michelangelo.

Nancy M. Fisher

Michaelangelo's Pietas

Milan, Florence, Rome

To find Christ in the stone the master followed fragments:
In Milan a ruin, broken, its arm detached and frayed.
The guide called the second modern,
Christ's features clear, but his friends in rough chiseled stone.

Bitter at ninety he stripped a yellow marble,
found Joseph of Arimathea, ageless as death the mirror,
holding the lifeless weight slumped in his arms.

Only a young world admires a young man's vision:
Salt white restored, guarded from madmen with axes,
the polished mother is massive yet seems so fragile
across her lap the man-child weightless lies.

The Bread of Life

John 6: 35, 41-51

The preacher read: *I am the bread of life ...*
and there were murmurs: *This is but a man.*
We know his father, Joseph, the one who ran
the Nazareth carpentry shop. How's he to lift
man's spirits? What nonsense is this about blood and bread?
The preacher said: *What must we make of this?*
How some may understand, while others miss
the message—blind or deaf, as good as dead.
The preacher said: *Perception is the key,*
that's Blake, but Matthew has another clue:
become as children, open your clouded eyes—see
the kingdom of God revealed to those who knew
Jesus as John would see him. Hush! Did you hear?
A child's voice, "Daddy" whimpers through the air.

Nancy M. Fisher
The Prodigal

Two Portraits by de Chirico
"The Prodigal Son", Milan 1922

1

This is the famous one,
       a mannequin,
       a faceless robot,
       a puppet.
The father is a statue,
       but his head is bowed
       and he wears a suit.
His son, despite his wooden legs,
       has human feet,
and his hand rests kindly on his father's shoulder.
What is his father giving him?
A kite-like thing of paper,
       maybe a plane.
The son, for all his facelessness,
       is brilliant in his optimism—
       blue and orange—
backed by the hills of Italy and flanked
       by arches of the Renaissance.
There is no second brother.
God is dead.

2

       "The Return of the Prodigal Son"
       San Francisco 1929
Who would have thought it? The images have changed.
The son stands humble behind his seated father.
Faceless still, his body is only human,
draped like a statue worthy of a Greek.
It is the father who is horribly changed.
Where is the kindly statue, marble benevolence?

Flame Dancer

Here is a seated figure, skeletal even,
his arms and legs encapsulated in rigid brick.
The very soul is wooden, and on his head,
the top hat of a circus clown.

No, it is Emily's gentleman Death stripped of his carriage.
DeChirica took his faith from Nietzsche, and his form.
He did not think to look outside the canvas.
Isn't the elder brother out there somewhere, I wonder?
And would he be mannequin, or like his brother, human?

Nancy M. Fisher
Flying Blind

Consider flying blind, under the hood.
Radar and radio become our guide
and in the cockpit, all the instruments should
agree, the ILS a needle wide.
How better to negotiate the rain
or find an altitude bereft of ice.
The charts for VFR depict terrain
but IFR approaches are precise.
Our ears deceive us with their tiny lies,
disorienting all within our cube.
Trust the altimeter, beware internal ice
in the carburetor or the pitot tube.
Lest we should fear or fabricate our fall,
let us fly sightless faith, as blind as Paul.

The Gulls

Kingston, Tennessee

Each spring the gulls come, following the river bed
between the Smokies and the Cumberlands;
the lakes are nearly dry, soggy as tide-
stripped marshes, naked as scalloped sea-soaked sands.
Why do they come? The robins signal spring;
the dempster dumpsters host the crows year round.
The ducks float unmolested; the wild geese wing
formations blasting a cacophony of sound.
In my mind's eye I see the ocean's surge:
Sandpipers flitting in the froth, white crabs
hiding from sunlight, slithering out to merge
with starlight. Surely even as a white gull stabs
at fishes, God's spirit snares us, bidding love and sing.
Leave winter to the crows, praise gulls in spring.

Nancy M. Fisher
Ash Wednesday

A soldier, wounded, needing a tourniquet,
is marked in blood, a T upon his forehead.
It is the mark, a deed of comradeship;
each soldier coming after knows the dead
can wait, if they but let the blood to flow
and tighten it again.
                       And so tonight
we too are marked—with ashes—before we go
about our tasks these several weeks, in spite
of all our sins, our failings, our hidden dark
secrets. A cross, it signals visibly;
nor sacraments, nor sprinklings leave a mark.
This to the world we show forth solemnly.
So let us be ambassadors for Christ,
emerging like ghosts before the Holy mist.

About the Author

Nancy McWhorter Fisher is a former English professor, having taught at Tennessee Wesleyan College for many years. Before that, she was one of the founding faculty at Roane State Community College. She has published in *Wind*, *Apalachee Quarterly*, and other journals. She was the featured poet in 1984 in *Teaching English in the Two Year College*. Her previous books include a chapbook, *Witnessing* (1988), and *Vision at Delphi* (1995). Professional articles appeared in *Teaching English in the Two Year College* and *Journal of Psychological Type*.

As an undergraduate at Woman's College UNC (now UNC-Greensboro), she studied under Randall Jarrell. Poets, he said, stand in the rain waiting to be hit by lightning. She has been blessed with gentle rain, only occasional lightning. What Jarrell gave to his students, she has labored to pass on to hers—a love of poetry. After an MA from Florida State University, she finished her doctorate at UT-Knoxville, writing her dissertation on Jarrell. She is married to William D. Fisher, former Oak Ridge biologist turned optometrist. Their son, Karl, teaches Spanish and their daughter, Karen, is an optician. Two grandsons, Bill and Zach, are just reaching adulthood. She currently lives with her husband in Kingsport, Tennessee.

About the Cover Artist

With degrees from Middle Tennessee State University and the Art Institute of Chicago, Julie Jack is an Associate Professor of Art at Tennessee Wesleyan College in Athens, Tennessee. Her work may be viewed at http://Web.mac.com/JulieJack.

www.ingramcontent.com/pod-product-compliance
Lightning Source LLC
Chambersburg PA
CBHW052108070526
44584CB00017B/2386